NEW VANGUARD 288

THE FRENCH 75

The 75mm M1897 field gun that
revolutionized modern artillery

STEVEN J. ZALOGA   ILLUSTRATED BY FELIPE RODRÍGUEZ

OSPREY PUBLISHING

Bloomsbury Publishing Plc

PO Box 883, Oxford, OX1 9PL, UK

1385 Broadway, 5th Floor, New York, NY 10018, USA

E-mail: info@ospreypublishing.com

www.ospreypublishing.com

OSPREY is a trademark of Osprey Publishing Ltd

First published in Great Britain in 2020

A catalogue record for this book is available from the British Library.

ISBN: PB 9781472839305; eBook 9781472839312

ePDF 9781472839282; XML 9781472839299

20 21 22 23 24   10 9 8 7 6 5 4 3 2 1

Index by Fionbar Lyons
Typeset by PDQ Digital Media Solutions, Bungay, UK
Printed and bound in India by Replika Press Private Ltd.

AUTHOR NOTE

Unless otherwise specified, the photos in this book are from the author's
collection.

CONTENTS

THE FRENCH 75

The 75mm M1897 field gun that revolutionized modern artillery

INTRODUCTION

The French Canon de 75 was a revolutionary step forward in field artillery design. It was popularly called 'notre glorieuse 75' (our glorious 75) or the 'soixante-quinze' (seventy-five). The French 75mm gun pioneered most of the innovations that would become typical of field artillery in the 20th century including a modern recoil system, fast-acting breech, smokeless powder, on-carriage sights, and single-piece ammunition. While some previous guns included one of these features, the 75mm M1897 combined them all in a highly effective design. All major armies began copying these features around the turn of the century, making the French 75mm the most influential gun of its era. Unlike most World War I weapons, the 75mm gun remained in widespread service in World War II. The basic gun and ammunition system remained viable, even if the gun required some improvements in its antiquated carriage. The French 75mm gun had been developed in an era of horse traction, so adapting it to motorized towing was the most important

Many Canon de 75 *modèle 1897* have been preserved. This example was on display for many years at the Ordnance Museum at Aberdeen Proving Ground, Maryland. The carriage is from Bourges 1919 production, the barrel is from Bourges 1917 production, and the shield is the later simplified four-piece type. (Author)

innovation of the interwar years. Both the German and American armies modified the 75mm into an expedient antitank gun, and it served in this role through 1945. Small numbers of 75mm guns remained in service in the backwaters of the French Empire well into the 1960s, and a small number soldier on as ceremonial saluting guns.

DEVELOPMENT

In the wake of the poor performance of French artillery in the 1870 Franco-Prussian War, the French Army was keen on adopting new technology to restore the technological balance. The first new divisional field gun since the war was the Schneider-Creusot Canon de 90mm *modèle 1877* developed by Col Charles Ragon De Bange, working at Société des anciens établissements Cail. This gun featured an interrupted screw-breech that incorporated De Bange's innovative obturator system to prevent propellant gases from leaking out of the breech during firing.

Many other technical innovations were taking place in French artillery design at this time. Verchère de Reffye, commander of the Meudon arsenal, fostered the use of single-piece fixed ammunition using a brass casing. In 1874, chemist Edmond Fremy pioneered the use of nickel steel in place of brass for the manufacture of gun barrels. In 1884, Paul Marie Vielle introduced a nitrocellulose smokeless powder, called Poudre B, that offered better range with smaller charges and greater safety than conventional black powder.

Gun recoil remained one of the enduring problems of field guns. When a field gun fired, it recoiled back several feet, forcing the crew to push it back into firing position and re-aim it against its target. Technologies for recoil abatement were in progress for large coastal and naval guns, but no system seemed suitably compact and effective for field guns. Early efforts at recoil systems included pneumatic, spring and hydraulic pistons. By the early 1870s, hydraulic buffers had appeared that reduced recoil but did not entirely eliminate it. These early recoil systems were plagued by fluid leakage when the gun fired. Artillery designers also began to add wheel-brakes and spades at the end of the carriage to lessen the effects of recoil, all with mixed results.

Capt Louis Baquet designed the first French guns equipped with a hydro-pneumatic recoil recuperator, the Obusier de 120mm C *modèle 1890* and the

The precursor to the Canon de 75 *modèle 1897* was the Canon de 90 *modèle 1877* De Bange. It introduced a more effective breech system but, like other contemporary guns, lacked a recoil system.

5

The two engineers most responsible for the design of the Canon de 75 were Joseph Albert Deport of Atelier de Puteaux on the right and Charles Sainte-Claire Deville of the Bourges foundry on the left.

Canon de 155mm C *modèle 1890*. These both used the Locard system in which the barrel recoiled inside a mandrel bearing the trunnions.

In 1889, Capt Charles Sainte-Claire Deville at the Bourges foundry developed a rapid-firing 52mm (2in) gun using a semi-automatic breech and a hydraulic recuperator. The Deville 52mm gun offered a rate of fire of about 30 rounds per minute compared to only about two rounds per minute for the 90mm De Bange gun. Deville subsequently designed a 57mm gun using a short hydro-pneumatic recoil system. He introduced a number of innovations on this gun including seats for the gun crew, an independent sight, a collimator (fixed telescope for direct fire) and a fuze setter to accelerate the preparation of projectiles for firing. Although this gun was not adopted for service, its innovations played an important role in the subsequent 75mm gun.

In 1889, the French Army sponsored the development of two 75mm guns, as technology demonstrators helped define the features needed for a future divisional gun. Capt Baquet's 75mm gun used a short recoil system, and one by Capt Ducros used a spade at the end of the carriage to minimize recoil, but lacked a recoil system. Neither was efficient enough to recommend serial production.

On January 21, 1891, a *Comité Technique de L'artillerie* was established by the director of artillery to develop the new-generation field gun. The basic characteristics included a calibre of 75mm, a weight of 1,100kg in the firing position, projectiles of about 7.5kg with an initial velocity of 600m/s, a fast-acting breech and extractor and a recoil system. A travel weight of 1,700kg including the gun and its caisson was imposed based on the tractive power of six horses of roughly 300kg each.

On February 22, 1892, the committee was made aware of two new patents by the German engineer Konrad Haussner for a novel hydro-pneumatic recoil system. He had originally been employed by the Krupp arsenal, but when the firm rejected the use of his innovation, he decided to patent it himself. Patent rights were subsequently acquired by the Gruson arsenal for their fortress artillery. In the meantime, Haussner also tried to sell his concept outside Germany, including filing patent applications in France. The Haussner recuperator was a long-recoil system using a piston within an oil-filled chamber interacting with a neighbouring air-filled chamber. When the gun fired, the air was compressed, and then expanded back, bringing the gun barrel back into the battery.

The committee discussed these patents with the artillery director at the Atelier de Puteaux (APX), Cdt Joseph Albert Deport. Hydro-pneumatic recoil systems were not entirely new, but had been plagued by air leakage problems when the gun fired. The artillery committee asked Deport whether he could design a hydro-pneumatic recoil system that did not infringe on the Haussner patent. He replied that he could do so, starting the development process.

The committee authorized work on four designs. The Deport gun with a long-recoil system was designated Canon C, and three other designs called Canons A, B and D were based respectively on designs by captains Baquet, Ducros and Locard. The other designs examined short-recoil systems as a back-up in case of the failure of the Deport's revolutionary long-recoil design.

One problem in French weapons' development was the independence of the several arsenals and foundries, all of which were intent on offering their own designs for any army requirement. Fortunately, during the gestation of the 75mm gun there was a particularly able succession of senior artillery commanders serving as the artillery director and leading the artillery committee. They managed to put a check on excessive and tangential engineering projects, while at the same time displaying the patience to allow promising designs to mature.

The Canon C was strongly influenced by Sainte-Claire Deville's earlier 57mm gun. To steady the gun, the carriage had both an earth spade at the rear of the carriage and a wheel-brake (*abattage*) that locked the wheels. These features, in combination with the innovative recoil system, were intended to make the Canon C entirely stable during the firing sequence. As a result, the gun could continue to fire multiple rounds in rapid succession without the need for the crew to move the gun back into position. This was a revolutionary improvement in field guns, offering a ten-fold increase in rate of fire from two rounds per minute to 20 rounds per minute. The Canon C incorporated a host of other innovations including a separate sight, seats for the gunner, and a gun-shield to protect the crew from shrapnel and small arms fire. The associated ammunition was modern in design, using fixed projectiles with a brass case and mechanical time fuzes. To accelerate the firing sequence, an automatic fuze setter was developed in place of the more conventional manual fuze wrench.

Trials of Deport's Canon C began at Mont-Valérien in October 1893. The initial design suffered from excessive loss of recoil fluid and proved capable of only about five rounds per minute compared to the requirement for 20 rounds per minute. Nevertheless, the gun offered great promise and so development continued after the recoil system underwent a complete redesign. In 1894, the French government bought production rights for the new Nordenfeldt eccentric breech for the 75mm gun programme. This breech operated much more quickly than previous types such as De Bange's design.

After being denied a promotion, at the end of 1894 LtCol Deport retired from the army and went to work for the Forges de Châtillon-Commentry. He was replaced in December 1894 by the talented artillery designer Charles

One of the innovations of the Canon de 75 *modèle 1897* was an automated fuze setter, the Débouchoir *modèle 1897*. This considerably sped up the preparation time of the ammunition. Instead of using a wrench to set the time on the projectile's mechanical time fuze, the ammunition loader would place the round nose-down into the fuze setter. It was mechanically programmed to set the right time based on the range and projectile type. The lever was used to set the fuze. The two brass cups could be pre-programmed for either the shrapnel or high-explosive round.

The Canon de 75 used a Nordenfeldt eccentric breech that revolved 155 degrees from the closed position on the left through to the open position on the right. When the gun fired, the brass casing was automatically ejected.

Sainte-Claire Deville who led the development of Canon C to completion. Another exceptional artillery designer, Capt Emile Rimailho, joined the team in January 1895.

Although the leak problem had abated to the point where it could fire 200 rounds before needing refilling, the artillery committee desired better performance. On the other hand, the most promising of the competing designs, such as Baquet's Canon B, was not especially stable after recoil and could only fire four shots per minute. The focus remained on the Canon C.

By 1895, there were two variations of the design under consideration, the Canon C1, very similar to the original Canon C and weighing 1,100kg without shields, and the lighter Canon C2, which also weighed 1,100kg but included 5mm steel shields to protect the crew.

APX delivered the first test battery of Canon C1 in 1895 for examination by the Bourges Commission, for field tests at the Châlons camp during summer manoeuvres, and for operational tests by the 15e Brigade at Nimes. The 1895 tests were satisfactory enough that the artillery committee recommended production of a further 54 guns in order to equip three artillery groups for further field trials.

Continued problems with recuperator leaks prompted Sainte-Claire Deville to redesign the recuperator again, called the Frein *modèle II*. A new diaphragm prevented the hydraulic fluid from leaking into the compressed air piston. This permitted an increase of pressure in the air piston and also assured that the recuperator fully returned the gun tube to battery after each firing. The first of these was built in February 1896 and sent for trials in August–September 1896.

There was some pressure on the committee to approve the Canon C for serial production since Germany had adopted a new 77mm field gun in 1896. Due to the enormous investment that was entailed in re-equipping the French Army's divisional artillery, the committee wanted to make certain it was buying the best possible gun and urged patience.

In 1896, there were field trials pitting the Canon C against the experimental Canon B3 and the older 90mm De Bange gun. The trials concluded that a Canon C battery would overwhelm a battery of Canon B3 or 90mm De Bange gun in three minutes or less while suffering only a third of the losses. Furthermore, a Canon C battery engaged against two batteries of either the 80mm or 90mm De Bange guns would disable half the opposing guns at a loss of only a third of its own guns.

One detail examined in 1896 was the paint finish of the gun. Two colours were tested, pearl grey and olive green. Although the green offered better

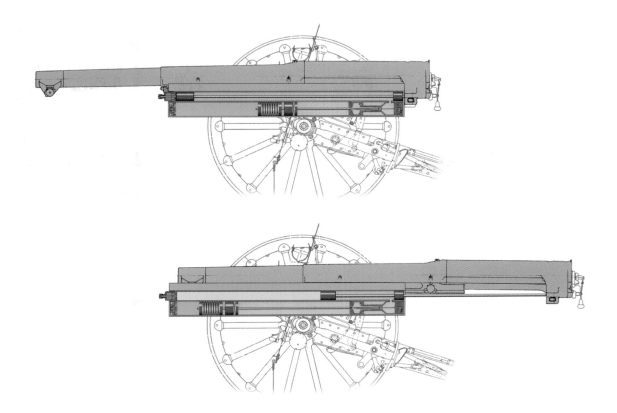

camouflage, there was some concern that in sunny summer weather, the ammunition *caisson* would become overheated by sunlight. The pearl grey was more reflective than the green but the formal decision to adopt the grey colour was not taken until after another set of trials at the Châlons camp in 1897.

Trials in 1897 confirmed the effectiveness of the new Frein *modèle II* recuperator design. Field trials favoured the use of three four-gun batteries per regiment rather than two six-gun batteries. The artillery committee reported in November 1897 that the Canon C2 was ready for service use. The Canon C2 was formally adopted by the war ministry on March 28, 1898. The weapon system, including the associated limbers, was designated as Matériel de 75 *modèle 1897* while the gun itself was designated as Canon de 75 *modèle 1897*.

The Canon de 75 received unusually strong parliamentary support. The adoption of a new German field gun in 1896 and the obvious obsolescence of the 90mm De Bange convinced French politicians to support unanimously a special budgetary procedure to fund its manufacture. Initial authorization for the production of a first tranche of 340 guns had been approved in 1895 even before trials had been completed. About a hundred 75mm gun barrels were completed at the Bourges arsenal in 1896. On December 4, 1896, the Puteaux workshops had been authorized to begin construction of 600 carriages and assemblies for the 75mm gun. As a result, by April 1898, a month after its official adoption, there were 220 75mm M1897 guns in service.

The illustration above shows the operation of the recuperator system on the Canon de 75. The upper chamber of the recuperator contained hydraulic fluid (yellow) which flowed into the lower chamber through a throttle valve system. Compressed nitrogen (blue) was contained in the forward portion of the lower chamber, separated from the fluid by diaphragms. When the gun fired, the hydraulic fluid in both upper and lower chambers momentarily compressed the nitrogen forward as shown in the lower illustration depicting full recoil. This also opened a valve which allowed ordinary air temporarily into the forward part of the upper chamber. The extremely compressed nitrogen then expanded back to its previous volume, returning the gun barrel to battery. (Author)

A 75mm gun for the horse artillery

Until the adoption of the 75mm M1897 gun, the French Army had deployed two field guns, the 90mm De Bange for the infantry divisions, and the lighter 80mm De Bange for horse batteries (*batteries à cheval*). The 75mm M1897 was obviously lighter and superior to the 80mm De Bange, and so horse batteries began receiving this weapon as a provisional replacement. Once in service, there was some debate as to whether a lighter version of the 75mm gun might be preferable. The production version of the gun weighed 1,205kg, somewhat greater than the original 1,100kg requirement. A programme to examine this issue began in 1902. Various alternatives were considered including a 65mm gun, a rapid-fire 70mm gun and a rigidly mounted 75mm gun. One of the alternatives offered in 1904 by Capt Roy was a 75mm gun using a shorter barrel and a revised recoil system. Trials of this gun in 1905 led to a decision in 1906 to abandon any further development. A subsequent proposal was to attempt to lighten the 75mm M1897 gun, and to lower overall system weight by reducing the stowage in the ammunition caissons. Test examples of this configuration were subjected to field trials in 1908 but eventually rejected. In 1912, the cavalry adopted the Schneider *modèle PD 13 bis*, based on the earlier PD 13 that had been developed for a Russian Army requirement. This weighed 960kg when deployed and fired the same ammunition as the Canon de 75 *modèle 1897*. A small number were in service at the start of the war; an order for 12 more batteries followed in September 1914 and another for 200 additional guns in May 1915.

A related type, the Schneider PD 7, had been ordered by Greece before the war but not delivered. These 32 guns were delivered to the French Army in May 1915. Mexico ordered eight batteries of the Canon de 75mm TR Saint-Chamond, totalling 48 guns, in 1902, and this was followed by later orders to increase the total to 20 batteries. Remaining portions of these contracts were cancelled in November 1914 due to the war and in May 1915 the French Army agreed to purchase 200 of these guns. Some of these were diverted to use on the initial version of the Saint-Chamond tank in 1916.

Improvements to the 75mm gun

Once the 75mm gun reached widespread service, there was a succession of attempts to introduce improvements. There were several efforts starting in 1900 to improve the wheel lock system since it was found that the gun tended to shift when fired from uneven or broken ground. Although several proposals were studied through 1909, none were adopted.

Gun crews in North Africa complained that the splinter shield was inadequate when facing snipers. As a result, an improved gun-shield, the 'Bouclier Type Afrique,' was adopted in limited numbers in 1902. There had been similar complaints in metropolitan France that the original splinter shield on the gun was not as comprehensive as on its German counterpart. In 1909, the Section Technique offered a modest improvement based on the 1902 African type which extended the coverage between the right and left

A **CANON DE 75 *MODÈLE 1897***

This general arrangement drawing shows the standard wartime version of the Canon de 75 *modèle 1897* with the improved seven-piece shield adopted in 1909. The Canon de 75 was generally painted in pearl grey, though camouflage paint began to be applied to many guns in the later years of the war.

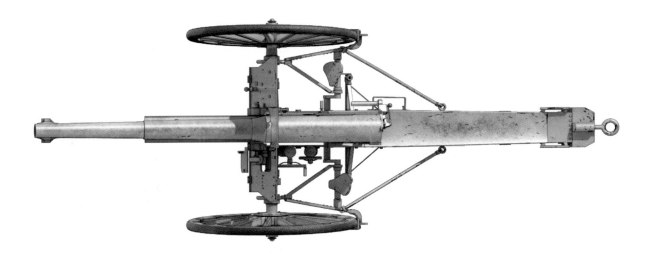

A Canon de 75 *modèle 1897* during the September 1908 manoeuvres. This is an early production example of the gun with the initial split splinter shields as well as the early pattern wheels. Some but not all of these older guns were modified after 1909 with an additional plate between the two upper shields, plus aprons below the main shields.

shield over the gun and added a lower apron. This modification was tested in Tulle in 1909–10 and subsequently adopted as an upgrade on older guns and as a standard feature on new-production guns in the autumn of 1910.

There were also complaints about the durability of the spoked wheels. The original wheel was composed of 14 wooden spokes connected to a wooden wheel made of seven segments with an outer steel rim. A variety of improvements were examined starting in 1903. A strengthened type added a steel reinforcement where the spokes met the wheel segments and it was adopted in November 1913 as the 'Roues no 7 renforcée.' A third type was later adopted as the no 7C which had only two wooden wheel segments instead of seven.

By 1903, there had been some concerns about the flanges on the gun mount suffering from stress cracks. Improvements were introduced in 1907, and the improved types were designated as the Affûts de 75 *modèle 1897–1907*. There were a number of other small changes made before the war, including the use of a new mount for an improved gun sight in 1901.

Prewar 75mm fortress guns

After the standardization of the 75mm gun in 1898, there were several programmes to adapt the gun to other roles. The first of these began in 1899 to adapt the gun to coastal defence. The configuration that was finally adopted was a circular concrete platform with a special traverse frame with a central pivot attached to the undercarriage that made it simpler for the crew to rapidly traverse the gun. Ten of these were deployed at Dunkirk and Calais.

There were two separate efforts to adapt the 75mm gun to fortresses. The basic type for firing through an embrasure replaced the wheels and axle with a traversing frame attached to the concrete floor. A total of 92 guns were deployed in 46 Casemates de Bourges. Efforts to adapt the 75mm gun to armoured turret mounts found that the gun tube was too long to fit existing turret types. As a result, a special version of the 75mm gun was developed with a shortened barrel for this role.

75mm antiaircraft guns

Efforts to develop a version with higher elevation to shoot at Zeppelins began in 1905. An improvised mount using an ordinary 75mm gun was tested at the Mailly proving ground in 1907. The initial platform configuration was similar to the coastal gun mount except that a central concrete pylon formed the basis for the gun position, enabling the gun to be mounted on a steel frame at a sufficiently high elevation. In 1911, the Platforme de Toul was adopted for this role. Five sections of 75mm guns were deployed on these mounts for the defence of Paris shortly before the outbreak of the war. Improvised versions of this type of mounting were adopted during the war by front-line units to deal with German observation balloons.

The Platforme de Toul *modèle 1911* was cumbersome, and led to the development of a much smaller steel frame design by APX that was adopted as the Platforme demi-fixé de 75 *modèle 1915*. These first went into combat in March 1915 around Verdun and Dunkirk. By 1918, some 459 of these had been built, with 158 assigned to the defence of Paris out of a total of 600 on order.

While the platform mounts were acceptable when engaging slow-moving aerial targets such as dirigibles, the growing role of fixed-wing aircraft led to interest in a more sophisticated mounting that could rapidly track and engage moving aircraft. LtCol Sainte-Claire Deville, then head of the Châlons artillery proving ground, began a programme in February 1908 to develop such a weapon. Two different configurations of this mounting were eventually developed, a semi-mobile trailer mounting (*rémorque*) and a self-propelled version (*auto-canon*) on a De Dion Bouton truck. A prototype of the truck version was completed first in 1910 for trials at Châlons. The gun mount was not sufficiently stable so a set of outriggers was added for the 1911 trials. Besides the gun vehicle itself, an associated ammunition vehicle (*auto-caisson*) was also built, carrying 180 rounds of 75mm ammunition. Trials were conducted on the coast near Toulon and Calais in 1912, firing against target gliders towed behind fast destroyers. These tests were successful enough that the two vehicles were accepted for service in 1913 as the Auto-canon de 75 *modèle 1913*.

Delays were caused by some committee members suggesting that a tracked chassis would be better. Tests found this not to be the case, and in the event, the De Dion Bouton was finally approved as the chassis

By far the most common of the static antiaircraft versions of the 75mm gun was the Plate-forme demi-fixé de 75 *modèle 1915*. This was usually mounted in a concrete pit with a central pivot, permitting complete traverse. This particular example was photographed near Salonika on the Macedonian frontier during the campaign there in 1917.

The Auto-canon de 75 De Dion Bouton *modèle GM* was the final production type of the antiaircraft gun, and used the later chassis with an armoured hood.

France supplied 12 of the Auto-canon de 75 De Dion Bouton *modèle GM* to Poland in 1919 along with the accompanying *auto-caisson* seen here on parade after the 1920 Russo-Polish War. They served with the 3rd Battalion, 1st AntiAircraft Regiment and in the late 1930s were modernized by transferring the equipment to the modern Polski-Fiat 621 L trucks.

for the gun vehicle. Other chassis were examined for the *auto-caissons*, though again the De Dion Bouton became the standard type. As a result of these delays, the April 1913 order for 20 sets of equipment from APX did not take place until November 1914 when the first two were delivered. At the time, a section consisted of two *auto-canons*, two *auto-caissons* and a truck to carry additional crew and equipment.

The first *auto-canon* section, equipped with prototype guns, was attached to the 13e Régiment d'artillerie based in Vincennes. It was originally used to defend the General Headquarters (GHQ) at Vitry-Le François. In September 1914, the first gun was sent to Antwerp to help defend the city against Zeppelin attacks. The first serial production *auto-canons* were sent to defend the HQ of the Xe Armée in the Dunkirk area.

The army requirements continually increased, with a total of 160 sets on order by the war's end. The vehicles were complicated and expensive and there were 42 available at the start of 1917, 70 at the start of 1918 and 100 at the end of the war. The initial vehicles were mounted on the De Dion Bouton *modèle FZ*, the second batch on the *modèle GO* and the third on the *modèle GM*. During the war, 41 *sections des auto-canons* were deployed in combat and were credited with downing 269 aircraft and balloons. A total of 30 *auto-canons* were destroyed during the fighting. Besides their combat use in France, 18 *auto-canons* were deployed with the Armée française d'Orient in Greece and Bulgaria.

The semi-mobile version of the 75mm antiaircraft gun was accepted for service in 1917 as the Canon de 75 sur remorque *modèle 1917*. It closely resembled the rear portion of the *auto-canon* but lacked the engine and powertrain. This was considerably less expensive than the *auto-canon* and was viewed as significantly superior to the previous platform mounts. A total of 450 were ordered but only about 40 were in service when the war ended.

Small numbers of *auto-canons* were also provided to Allied armies. The Zeppelin raids against London led to a request for dispatch of some of these weapons, with the first delivered in September 1915, and the first action against a Zeppelin on October 13, 1915. In total, four *auto-canons* and one *auto-caisson* were provided to Britain, serving with the Royal Navy's Mobile Anti-Aircraft Brigade. Additional *auto-caisson* vehicles were constructed

B **VOITURE-CAISSON *MODÈLE 1897***

The combination of the limber and caisson together was called the Voiture-caisson *modèle 1897*. The limber for the Canon de 75 was the Avant-train *modèle 1897*. It carried 24 rounds of ammunition beneath the seats. This illustration omits the rack for the crew's rucksacks which was usually removed to gain access to the ammunition. The ammunition caisson, called the Arrière-train de caisson *modèle 1897*, carried 72 rounds of ammunition. Additional equipment for the gun was also stowed in the various compartments, including the fuze setter.

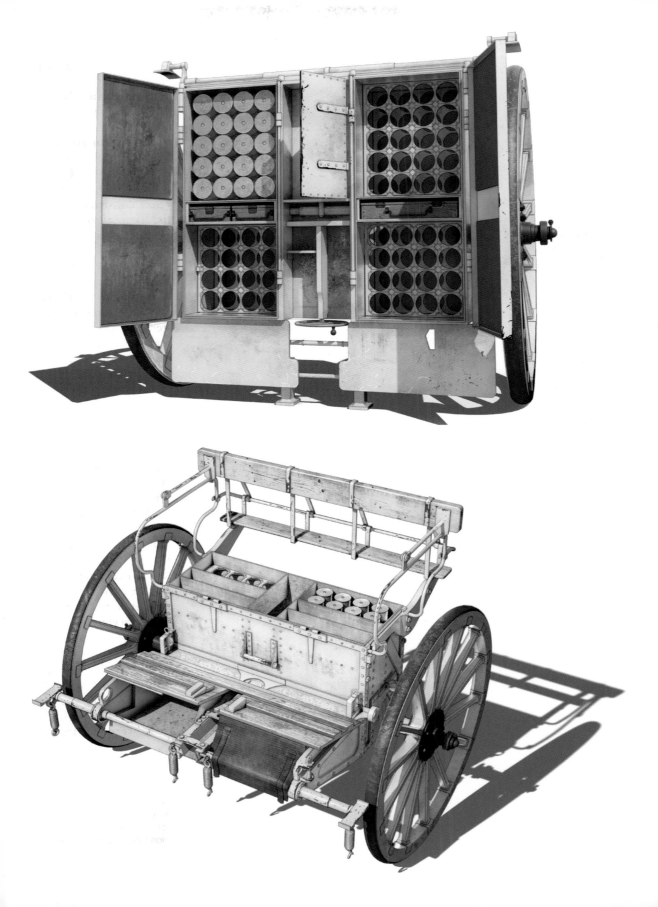

The Canon de 75 sur remorque *modèle 1917* entered production at the end of the war as a less expensive alternative to the *auto-canon*. The system is basically identical to that found on the *auto-canon*, but mounted on a trailer rather than a vehicle.

at the Coventry Ordnance Works using Lancia trucks. France also provided a further 35 75mm platform guns for fixed-site defence.

COMBAT USE OF THE CANON DE 75MM M1897

The Canon de 75mm *modèle 1897* was revealed to the public at a Bastille Day parade in Paris in 1899. The first hint of its capabilities came during the Boxer Rebellion in China in 1900. The French expeditionary force sent there included the 13e Batterie, 20e Régiment d'artillerie, commanded by Capt Edouard Jucqueau. The superior performance of the Canon de 75mm, especially its rapid-fire capability, created quite a sensation among other European forces, most notably the German detachments. The German Army, which had adopted a new 77mm gun in 1896, suddenly realized it was obsolete. Several armies began steps to develop new light field guns with modern recoil systems in the hopes of catching up with the French. Germany decided to upgrade its new 77mm FK 96 by adopting a long-recoil system, fixed ammunition and a new Rheinmetall sliding breech, designated as the Feldkanone 96 n.A (neuer Art). This gun, although significantly better than the 1896 gun, was still inferior to the French Canon de 75 in most respects. The French 75mm had a faster rate of fire, more potent high-explosive (HE) charge, superior range, and higher initial muzzle velocity. The French Army believed that its four-gun batteries were superior in firepower to the German six-gun batteries due to the technical advantages of the 75mm gun.

Comparative technical data		
	Canon de 75 *modèle 1897*	**77mm FK 96 n.A**
Crew	7	5
Length (m)	4.45	3.28
Width (m)	1.51	1.53
Barrel length (calibres)	L/36	L/27
Deployed weight (kg)	1,140	1,020
Elevation	-11° to +18°	-13° to +15°
Traverse	6°	7°
Rate of fire (rpm)	20–30	10
Maximum range (km)	11.1	8.4
HE projectile weight (kg)	5.5	6.8
Projectile HE fill (kg)	0.78	0.19
Initial velocity (m/s)	575	465

At the outbreak of war in August 1914, France possessed 4,780 Canons de 75mm of which 3,792 were deployed with the northeast field armies in 948 batteries. Of these, 405 batteries were with the active divisions. Each division had 36 guns in three groups (12 guns per group), each of three batteries (four guns per battery). Each cavalry division had a group with three batteries. There were an additional 252 75mm batteries in the Régiments de corps d'armée (RAC) with each regiment having four groups with 48 guns. The remaining guns were in reserve divisions (225 batteries), territorial divisions (60 batteries), fortifications (32 batteries) and North African units (46 batteries). On average, each gun was allotted 1,390 rounds of ammunition, about 40 percent explosive and 60 percent shrapnel.

Krupp created the 7.7cm Flak L/35 (französisch) by re-boring captured Canon de 75 modèle 1897 to fire German 7.7cm ammunition. These were put on a specialized carriage to increase their elevation. About 345 conversions were assembled. They were often mounted on concrete pedestal mounts with central steel pivots for better traverse and elevation.

The Field Service Regulations of December 2, 1913 stated that 'Artillery no longer prepares attacks, it supports them.' During the opening battles along the frontiers, the Canon de 75 proved to be the best field gun in service. Indeed, both sides were very surprised at the lethality of modern field guns. For example, on August 7, 1914, the German 2.Badisches Dragoner-Regiment Nr.21, deployed along a tree-line northeast of Verdun, was virtually wiped out by the 6e Batterie, 42e RAC firing from a range of 5,400m. On August 19, 1914, two groups of the 5e RAC destroyed 18 German 77mm guns in a few minutes from a range of 3,200m, killing about 300 horses and killing or wounding most of the German gun crews.

The French 75mm gun was part of a broader trend in firepower that also included the modern machine gun. The combination of these new, fast-firing weapons swept the horse cavalry from the modern battlefield and severely limited the ability of the infantry to conduct traditional attacks. For the infantry to survive on the modern battlefield, field entrenchment became essential.

Rebellion in France. This is a Canon de 75 in action in Morocco after the 1911 Agadir crisis with one ammunition caisson to the left of the gun and another in the foreground. This is an early configuration gun with the split shields.

The French Army quickly realized that prewar doctrine was unsuitable and that new tactics had to be instituted immediately. Whereas the artillery had previously been viewed as an ancillary service, it quickly became apparent that its use was central to the modern battlefield. For example, on

A French 75mm battery in the opening phase of the conflict. The Canon de 75 and its limber were towed by a six-horse team. This is the early configuration of the gun with the initial type of splinter shield.

August 13, 1914, Gen Augustin Dubail ordered the 1ère Armée that 'Every attack must be prepared by the guns, after which they continually support the infantry's effort.'

It also became apparent that the French Army's high esteem for the 75mm gun had blinded them to the need for heavier weapons with greater range. With the advent of field telephones and observation techniques, field artillery was no longer confined to the direct-fire mission, but could undertake fire missions beyond the line-of-sight. The 75mm gun was designed primarily for a direct-fire mission and was not well suited to engaging targets beyond the line-of-sight due to its limited elevation. The German Army, dismayed by the technical superiority of the French 75mm gun, had responded by adding 105mm gun batteries to their divisional regiments. These were very well suited to counter-battery fire against French 75mm gun units. Army chief Gen Joseph Joffre noted on August 24, 1914 that 'The German artillery is out of the reach of our 75, which are unable to neutralize it.' It took the French Army several years to catch up with the German Army in terms of heavy guns.

A side-by-side comparison of the French Canon de 75 *modèle 1897* on the left and the German 77mm Feldkanone 96 n.A on the right.

The crisis of the 75

Prewar planning also failed to appreciate the enormous ammunition consumption rates of field artillery. French units consumed about half of the available stocks in the first month of fighting and nearly all the prewar supply by October 1914. A crash programme was begun to increase production with the prewar daily capacity of 10,000 rounds increasing to about 32,000 by December 1914, 63,000 by January 1915 and 70,000 by June 1915.

Mechanizing the 75mm gun

One of the main problems with the 75mm gun was the lack of modern wheels and suspension which prevented motorized towing. In the 1920s, the French Army experimented with the use of slow agricultural tractors to tow the 75mm gun. The Atelier de Fabrication in Vincennes revived the idea of a trailer to carry the 75mm gun, towed behind a Latil TL truck. Citroën-Kégresse was aware of this problem as it affected most artillery pieces of the era. In hopes of winning export contracts, the firm developed a 'train rouleur' that consisted of a pair of bogies, each with two wheels, that could be clipped underneath the axle of a field gun. The 50cm steel wheels had a rubber rim and were connected by a simple spring. In the process of attaching the bogie, the gun's original spoked wheels were elevated off the ground. The Citroën bogie permitted motorized towing at speeds of 15–20km/h. This system was intended to be used in conjunction with Citroën-Kégresse half-tracks as the prime movers.

In 1928, the French Army conducted a series of motorization trials to compare the Vincennes trailers and Citroën-Kégresse bogies. The trailers were rejected as being too large and heavy. On December 4, 1929, the army ordered 180 sets of the Citroën-Kégresse bogies as part of a larger programme to motorize seven infantry and three cavalry divisions. Service use of the bogies found that they were cumbersome to attach and detach, slowing artillery deployment in the field.

In 1934, another set of trials were conducted using modified 75mm guns fitted with Michelin and Dunlop pneumatic tires. After improvements were made, the Michelin DS 270 x 28 tires were adopted in 1938 as the Roues No 11. About 700 of the 4,500 75mm guns available in 1940 were modernized with these wheels. The usual prime movers were the P 107 half-track or Laffly S 15 TL truck.

The shortage of modern antitank guns led the French Army to adopt the Canon de 75 as a stop-gap until the new 47mm gun appeared. The wartime Filloux mount was too crude, so a new traverse system was sought. Three firms offered circular platforms that attached under the Canon de 75 for quick traverse. In 1935, the Arbel design was selected as the Plate-forme métallique *modèle 1935* and a thousand of these were ordered in 1936. They were deployed in the Batteries divisionnaires anti-char (BDAC: divisional antitank battery) for the protection of light artillery regiments. They were also issued in small numbers to the normal gun batteries in the divisional artillery regiments. Most of the Canon de 75mm *modèle 1897–1933* were also deployed in the BDAC during the 1940 campaign.

The construction of the Maginot Line in the 1920s led to the development of a large number of specialized fortification mounts for the 75mm gun.

French Navy coastal defences frequently used the Canon de 75 *modèle 1897* on special pedestal mounts for faster traverse. This example was part of the defences of the port of Toulon and, in German hands, took part in the defence of Toulon against Free French units of the 1ère Division d'infanterie de marche during the fighting there in late August 1944 after the Operation *Dragoon* landings on the Mediterranean coast.

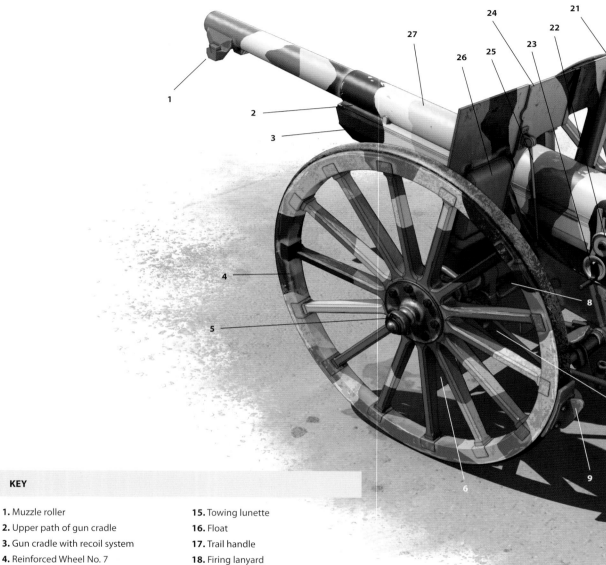

KEY

1. Muzzle roller
2. Upper path of gun cradle
3. Gun cradle with recoil system
4. Reinforced Wheel No. 7
5. Wheel cap
6. Armoured apron shield
7. Rocker arm
8. Axle
9. Brake pad (travel position)
10. Breech lever
11. Guard
12. Tie rod for brakes
13. Trail
14. Recoil spade

15. Towing lunette
16. Float
17. Trail handle
18. Firing lanyard
19. Firing hammer
20. Gun breech
21. Aiming device leather pouch
22. Range scale
23. Elevation crank
24. Armoured shield
25. Shield brace
26. Leather case for optical instruments
27. Gun tube

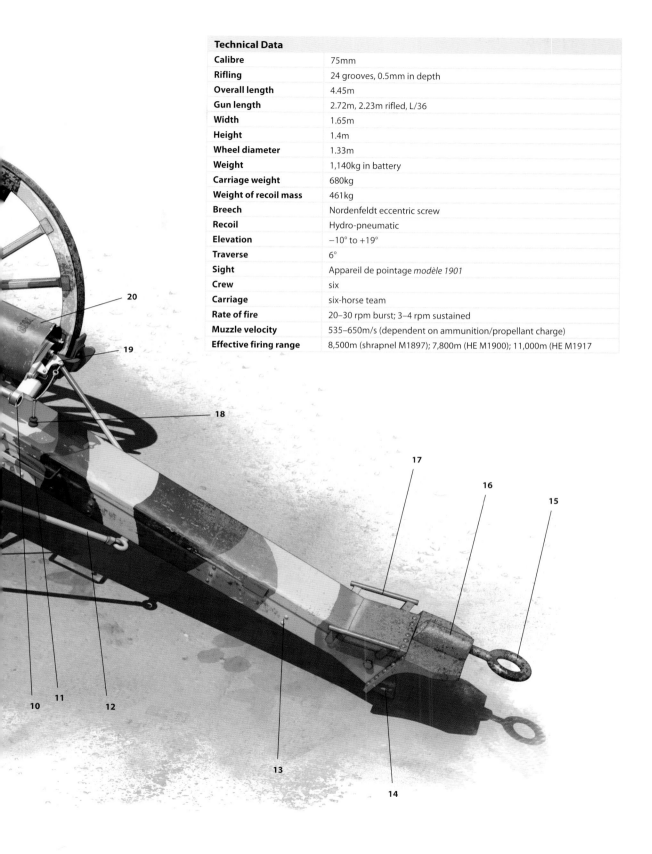

Technical Data	
Calibre	75mm
Rifling	24 grooves, 0.5mm in depth
Overall length	4.45m
Gun length	2.72m, 2.23m rifled, L/36
Width	1.65m
Height	1.4m
Wheel diameter	1.33m
Weight	1,140kg in battery
Carriage weight	680kg
Weight of recoil mass	461kg
Breech	Nordenfeldt eccentric screw
Recoil	Hydro-pneumatic
Elevation	−10° to +19°
Traverse	6°
Sight	Appareil de pointage *modèle 1901*
Crew	six
Carriage	six-horse team
Rate of fire	20–30 rpm burst; 3–4 rpm sustained
Muzzle velocity	535–650m/s (dependent on ammunition/propellant charge)
Effective firing range	8,500m (shrapnel M1897); 7,800m (HE M1900); 11,000m (HE M1917

20

19

18

17

16

15

10 11 12

13

14

THE AMERICAN 75MM GUN M1897

This gun, No 13579, was the first field gun of the American Expeditionary Force to see combat on October 23, 1917 when gunner Corp Robert Braley of the 6th Artillery, 1st Division fired at a German battery near Xanrey in the Lorraine region of France. This shows the 75mm gun when it returned to the US Military Academy at West Point, New York in 1918. This gun is still preserved today in the post museum.

Prior to the entry of the United States into the Great War, the US Army was developing a new 3in gun Model 1916 to replace the antiquated Model 1902. Following the US declaration of war on April 6, 1917, British and French military missions visited the United States to coordinate military issues. When it was decided that the American Expeditionary Force (AEF) would serve alongside the French Army, the French delegation indicated that it could provide the AEF with 75mm M1897 guns starting in August 1917. This was quickly approved and on June 5, 1917, the US Army decided to shift its field gun ammunition from 3in to French 75mm as a means to standardize ammunition. By this stage, 35 3in Model 1916 guns had been completed and they were rebored to 75mm. In September 1917, Ordnance began to award contracts for the manufacture of forgings for the M1897 gun barrel intended for France as partial compensation for delivery of complete guns to the AEF.

By May 1917, the US Army requirement for 75mm guns was 1,576 guns. Development of the 75mm Model 1916 continued, and in December 1917, one was shipped to France for modification with a Saint-Chamond hydro-pneumatic recuperator. The plans were to eventually switch to this new gun since it featured split trails that permitted greater elevation than the French M1897 carriage, and it also had better traverse. However, the design was far from mature and on January 16, 1918, Col E. S. Hughes, chief of the artillery section of the Ordnance procurement division, recommended that existing contracts for manufacture of the Model 1916 carriage be converted to the manufacture of the French M1897. After consultation with the head of the AEF, Gen John Pershing, on February 8, 1918 Army Ordnance ordered the conversion of the carriage contracts.

French officials were sceptical that their secret recuperator could be manufactured in the United States, and there were discussions about the supply of French-manufactured recuperators. Some engineering plans for the French carriage were received in August 1917, but the plans were not complete until April 1918. The American firms assigned to manufacture

 MECHANIZING THE CANON DE 75

1. In 1929, the French Army ordered 180 sets of Citroën-Kégresse 'trains-rouleurs' bogies. These clipped underneath the existing axle, elevating the carriage and permitting high-speed towing. The standard prime mover for the Canon de 75 was the Citroën-Kégresse P 17 half-track as seen here. The bogies were never entirely satisfactory and were cumbersome to attach and remove.

2. In the mid-1930s, the issue of adapting the gun to high-speed traction was revisited and a variety of modern wheels examined. In the event, the Michelin DS 270 x 28 tires were adopted in 1938 as the Roues No 11. The usual prime mover at this time was the Unic P 107 half-track as seen here or the Laffly S 15 TL truck.

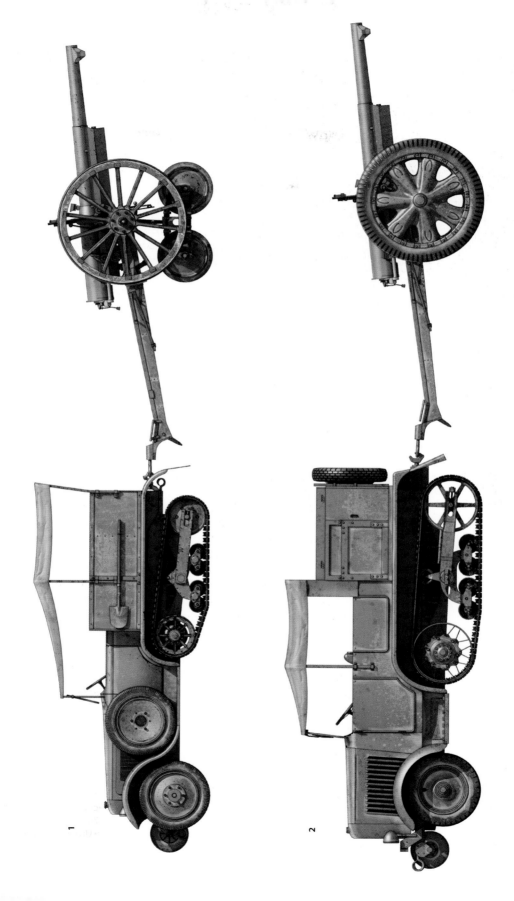

1

2

A battery of 75mm guns of the 6th Artillery, 1st Division near Exermont on October 4, 1918 during the Meuse–Argonne offensive.

the gun components had problems due to differences between French and American manufacturing practices, the metric measurement in use on the French guns and the lack of detailed tolerances on the drawings. It transpired that France had donated four worn-out Canon de 75 *modèle 1897* guns to Yale University for reserve officer training. In March 1918, Ordnance traded a battery of British 75mm guns for the Yale guns, providing immediate samples of a recuperator for detailed study. Further examples were obtained later from France. Examination of the recuperator design disclosed that its principal secret was that the precision machining of the initial forging required exceptionally well-trained craftsmen. On March 26, 1918, Singer Manufacturing Co was given a contract to manufacture 2,500 recuperators, followed by other contracts to Rock Island Arsenal, Ingersoll-Rand, and the French government.

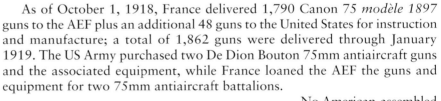

Production of 75mm Model 1897 Guns in the United States				
Product	Contractor	Orders	Complete Nov 11, 1918	Complete Apr 17, 1919
Gun carriage	Willys-Overland	2,927	291	1,299
Gun barrel	Symington-Anderson	4,300	103	860
Gun barrel	Wisconsin Gun	2,050	9	190

A 75mm M1897 gun assembled at Willys-Overland Co. in Toledo, Ohio in November 1918. The American-manufactured guns used the late simplified four-piece splinter shield.

As of October 1, 1918, France delivered 1,790 Canon 75 *modèle 1897* guns to the AEF plus an additional 48 guns to the United States for instruction and manufacture; a total of 1,862 guns were delivered through January 1919. The US Army purchased two De Dion Bouton 75mm antiaircraft guns and the associated equipment, while France loaned the AEF the guns and equipment for two 75mm antiaircraft battalions.

No American-assembled guns were completed before the war ended although 74 barrels, two recuperators, and 291 carriages had been accepted. Most of the wartime contracts were cancelled or curtailed after the war. In addition to the 1,862 guns delivered to the United States by France, a further 2,132 guns were completed in the United States for a grand total of 3,994 75mm M1897 guns.

Besides the American-designed Model 1916, Bethlehem Steel Company received a British contract to manufacture 268 18-pdr (3.3in) guns. This gun was also modified to fire 75mm ammunition, with the result that the US Army had three different 75mm guns in production at the end of the war. In the event, 124 of the British 75mm Gun Model 1917 were in transit to Europe at the end of the war and 34 75mm Gun Model 1916.

France provided the US Army with one caisson and one caisson limber per 75mm gun. The US requirement was for one caisson limber per gun plus three caissons and three caisson limbers to serve each gun. As a result, the US Army decided to manufacture its own gun caisson and gun carriage limber to make up for the shortfall as well as to serve with other 75mm guns that were in production including the 75mm Model 1916. US firms began the manufacture of 75mm ammunition in late 1917. By December 1918, about 15.4 million rounds had been produced.

One of the De Dion Bouton 75mm antiaircraft guns of the American Expeditionary Force, seen here in action near Montreuil, France on June 15, 1918 with Battery B, 1st AntiAircraft Battalion.

US Manufacture of French 75mm Ammunition 1917–Dec 1918 (in thousands)	
High explosive	5,586
Shrapnel	8,567
Gas	580
AA shrapnel	634
Total	**15,367**

Postwar US Army 75mm guns

The French 75mm M1897 gun remained the US Army's primary divisional field gun after World War I. There remained some interest in an improved weapon, particularly in regards to the carriage. A new design with a longer barrel and split-trail carriage was standardized in 1926 as the 75mm Gun M1, but there was no serial production due to a lack of funding. Development continued into the 1930s with the improved 75mm Gun M2, standardized in 1936. Once again, there was insufficient funding for serial production.

In 1933, army chief of staff Gen Douglas MacArthur ordered half of the army's light artillery to be motorized. The first motorization experiments began in 1931 at Fort Sill using a trailer developed by the Wichita Motor Company with pneumatic tires that could be fitted under the 75mm gun to permit its motorized towing. These were first

The initial stage in preparing the 75mm gun for motorized traction was the substitution of Martin Parry adaptors to the modernized M1897A4 carriage with modern pneumatic tires starting in 1932. As can be seen, the gun retained its original single trail.

75MM AMMUNITION

French 75mm ammunition followed a standard set of colouring and markings to avoid confusion over the many types of munitions. Generally, high explosive was painted yellow, shrapnel in red, chemical in medium green, practice in blue and inert/solid in black. As described below, there were variations on this system. The projectiles usually had markings indicating the type of filling, as well as the code for the workshop or arsenal which filled the projectile and the date of filling. This was important since some of these fillings could deteriorate due to time, humidity and temperature changes.

The basic marking on the brass case was located on the base and consisted of a simple identification of the ammunition type since this was all that was evident of the round when stowed in the caisson. Prewar cases often were stamped 75 de C (Canon de 75 Campagne) to distinguish 75mm field gun ammunition from mountain gun ammunition. Shrapnel casings were usually blank since they were the predominant type. High-explosive ammunition usually had a diagonal line across the base. As additional types of ammunition began to appear, a larger variety of markings had to be adopted. Basic high-explosive ammunition was painted with a single horizontal black band while the high-performance types such as the AL M1917 received two horizontal bands. Chemical rounds usually had a letter code indicating their fill. The sides of the cartridge had five or six lines of data stencilled near the base. The top line, nearest the base, indicated the charge and type of powder. The second line indicated the powder designation by lot, year and manufacturer. The third line indicated when and where the cartridge was filled. The fourth line gave in the initial muzzle velocity of the round in the form, for example, V_555 indicating *vitesse* (velocity = 555m/s). The fifth line indicated the shape of the casing/bore shape; in the case of the Canon de 75, it was code TL. Sometimes a sixth line was added indicating the primer type.

The descriptions of the ammunition illustrated here indicates the projectile type and the fuze depicted, generally the blunt impact fuze or the longer mechanical time fuze. A variety of fuzes could be fitted to the projectiles depending on the fire mission, so the illustrations here show a typical type of fuze, not all possible combinations.

A. Obus E (éclairant) (Illumination projectile E);+ Fusée-detonateur 24/31.

The illumination rounds had a white ogive and a grey body. The first line of text on the projectile simply identified the type of round. The second line indicated the filling arsenal and date. The star was a reminder that it was an illumination round.

B. Obus à balles avec balles lourde (Shrapnel projectile with heavy shot); + Fusée-detonateur 24/31.

Shrapnel ammunition with the heavy shot had a grey ogive and a red body. The markings consisted of the filling arsenal code on the first line and month and year of filling below.

C. Obus à balles avec charge arrière *modèle 1897–1917* (Shrapnel projectile with base charge); + Fusée-detonateur 24/31.

Shrapnel ammunition with a base charge was painted overall red with the top line indicating the filling arsenal and the second line giving the month and year when the projectile was filled. The 'Aéro' markings identify this as ammunition for antiaircraft guns.

D. Obus explosive *modèle 1900 N* (nitraté) (Explosive projectile M1900 N) + Fusée-detonateur percutantes de 24/31

The colouring for the high-explosive projectiles indicated the type of explosive fill. The markings on the ogive indicated the method of filling (first line); arsenal, month and year of filling (second line), designation of explosive (third and fourth lines). The marking on the body, either a horizontal line or circle, indicated the body type, monobloc or bi-bloc. A white cross above the copper band indicated the base configuration (*plaquette de culot*). One to four black crosses immediately above the copper driving band was a weight marking related to the propellant charges.

E. Obus explosif *modèle 1915 FN* en acier Bessemer (nitré), (Explosive projectile M1915 FN made from Bessemer steel, nitré explosive fill) + Fusée-detonateur percutantes de 24/31

The colouring on this round was overall yellow, indicating its high-explosive fill. The markings are otherwise the same as the previous projectile except for the white 'B' on either side of the projectile body which indicated a special type of steel used to manufacture the body (Bessemer or Thomas steels)

F. Obus explosive AL *modèle 1917* (Explosive projectile AL M1917) + Fusée-detonateur percutantes de 24/31

The marking on this round followed the usual practices with the first three lines indicating mode of filling, filling arsenal and date, and designation of explosive. The late-war AL projectile was manufactured from a steel/iron mix called 'Fonte acierée,' hence the 'FA' as the last line of text on the projectile body.

G. Obus fumigènes chargés en oléum et chlorhydrine sulfurique (Smoke projectile with Oleum/Chlorosulfuric acid) + Fusée-detonateur 24/31

Chemical projectiles were usually painted in overall green with various colour schemes to distinguish the types. Initially, smoke projectiles had a thick black band between the ogive and body of the projectile, but as seen here, the later pattern was to paint the entire ogive section of the projectile in black. The top line indicated the smoke filler Ph.F (Phosphore fondu) or O CS (oléum et chlorhydrine sulfurique). The second line indicated the filling arsenal and filling date.

H. Obus à toxiques persistants No 20 chargés en yperite (Gas projectile No 20 filled with Mustard gas) + Fusée-detonateurs 24/31

Chemical agent projectiles had a complicated set of coloured bands to indicate the type of chemical agent. Non-persistent gases had one or two white bands depending on their density. Persistent agents had one or two yellow-orange bands depending on whether they were slow-acting or fast-acting. The various type of chemical agents had code numbers, so for example No 12 was *lacrymogènes* (tear gas) while No 20 as depicted here was yperite/mustard gas. The main marking as seen here indicated the gas type.

The full modernization of the US Army's 75mm gun is shown in this example of the 75mm Gun M1897A2 on M2A3 carriage with M2 recoil system. The new carriage allowed high-speed towing as well as providing superior elevation and traverse for the gun.

A 75mm M1897A4 gun on the new split-trail carriage M2A2 of Battery A, 27th Field Artillery, 1st Armoured Division, deployed in an antitank role near the Castor railroad station on September 11, 1941 during the Louisiana manoeuvres.

tested in April 1931 using commercial Ford AA 1½ ton trucks. The trailer concept proved awkward and was rejected by the army. The designer Adolph Buquor, working for the Martin-Parry Corp in York, Pennsylvania, offered two different 'high-speed' designs for motorization of the 75mm gun in 1932, one using a double-wheel assembly and one proposing a simpler system with pneumatic tires. The simpler design was selected and first tested in February 1933. It was standardized on January 18, 1934 as the 75mm M1897A4 gun on carriage M1897A4. The Martin-Parry adapter required the use of a new axle, but following conversion, the gun could be towed up to speeds of 60 mph. The first conversion kits were delivered to 14 National Guard regiments in 1934. By 1941, 871 conversion kits had been authorized and about 605 conversions took place. The army eventually upgraded 56 of its 81 75mm batteries with this improved gun.

The 75mm M1897 still suffered from limited elevation and traverse, but these shortcomings required an entirely new carriage using split trails. This was derived from previous work on the 75mm Gun M2. The initial M2 carriage increased the elevation to 46 degrees and the traverse to 45 degrees right and 40 degrees left. It was fitted with a deployable jack to steady the gun during firing. The first production version was the M2A2 carriage which was procured starting in 1936. The improved M2A3 carriage was subsequently developed; it had shorter trail legs and curved segments inboard the wheels in place of the previous jack. By November 1941, 554 M2A2 and 188 M2A3 carriages had been accepted. Total conversions were about 1,400 guns.

A portion of these guns were deployed in divisional field artillery battalions, but some were issued with direct-fire sight for use as an expedient antitank gun. Under the October 1940 table of organization and equipment (TO&E), the 155mm howitzer battalion in each infantry division had an antitank gun battery with eight 75mm antitank guns. The army wanted to concentrate its antitank capabilities so on July 24, 1941, the War Department ordered the activation of an antitank battalion in each division. This battalion included the eight 75mm guns formerly in the 155mm battalion, reinforced by two more companies of the new 37mm antitank guns as they became available. In addition to the divisional battalions, the army began to form separate antitank battalions under GHQ control. Several of these were used in the Louisiana wargames in the autumn of 1941.

The US Army had decided to switch to the new 105mm howitzer as its principal

divisional field gun prior to World War II. However, the 75mm gun in its various forms remained in widespread service through 1943. The 75mm gun saw combat in small numbers during the Philippines fighting in December 1941. The 2/131st Field Artillery, equipped with the 75mm M1897A5 gun on carriage M2A3, was sent to the Philippines but diverted to Java in the Dutch East Indies. This was the only known combat use of this version by the US Army during World War II.

The large pool of surplus 75mm guns led to the decision in 1941 to mount them in half-tracks

Although the 75mm Gun M1897 had been largely replaced by the 105mm howitzer by 1943, some still remained in service for training purposes. This is a 75mm Gun M1897A4 on carriage M1897A4 with the Martin-Parry motorization adapter during exercises in England in September 1943.

as an expedient tank destroyer. The pilot T12 consisted of a M3 half-track carrier adapted to carry a M1897A5 75mm field gun. A trials batch of 36 T12s was ordered in July 1941 and subsequently standardized as the 75mm Gun Motor Carriage M3 on October 31, 1941. The initial production batches of this vehicle used the same shrapnel shield as the normal M2A3 gun carriage. This gave the crew limited protection, so in 1942 a new shield was developed that offered the crew better protection. The final production batch of the M3 employed the older 75mm M1897A5 gun on carriage M2A2 and was designated as 75mm GMC M3A1. A total of 2,202 M3 and M3A1 75mm GMC were completed by the time production ended in April 1943.

Fifty M3 75mm GMC saw combat use in the Philippines in December 1941 in three battalions of the Provisional Field Artillery Brigade. The M3 75mm GMC formed the heart of the new tank destroyer battalions created in the United States in 1942 and saw extensive combat in Tunisia in 1943. Some tank destroyer battalions retained the M3 75mm GMC at the time of Operation *Husky* on Sicily in July 1943. In late 1943, the army ordered 1,360 of the M3 tank destroyers to be converted back to M3A1

A mud-daubed M3 75mm GMC of the Anti-Tank Company, 39th Infantry Regiment, 9th Division sits in an ambush position in Kasserine Pass in March 1943.

half-track carriers, so that no more than 842 75mm M3 GMC were ever issued to the troops in their intended configuration. A handful of M3 75mm GMC were used in Ranger battalions in 1944, including the D-Day landings in Normandy. Although largely retired from service by the US Army by 1944, the M3 75mm GMC was still employed extensively by the US Marine Corps, starting with the Saipan campaign in the summer of 1944. Each Marine division had 12 M3 75mm GMC; in Marine service they were called self-propelled mounts (SPM) and were used for direct-fire support.

The M3 75mm GMC was not extensively exported through Lend Lease.

About 170 were provided to Britain where they were used mainly in the heavy troops of armoured car regiments. Their debut in British service occurred with the Royal Dragoons in Tunisia in 1943, and they were used extensively in Italy. A small number remained in service in France in 1944 but they were gradually retired through attrition. The Free French Army received M3 75mm GMC in Tunisia and six were used by the 4e Escadron, 9e Régiment de Chasseurs d'Afrique during the fighting in Tunisia in February–May 1943.

The British Army acquired 500 75mm M1897 guns from Bethlehem Steel in 1940 since the US government was restricted from arms sales due to neutrality legislation. In British service, the modernized guns with pneumatic tires were designated as Ordnance QF 75mm Mk 1*. This example is seen during training by Polish troops in Britain in 1941.

Finland acquired 48 Canon de 75 *modèle 1897* in 1940, locally calling them the 75 K 97. They were widely used for coastal defence like the example seen here at Järisevänniemi, north of Taipale on Lake Ladoga in September 1941. (SA-kuva/ CC-BY-4.0)

USE OF THE 75MM GUN IN WORLD WAR II

Britain

In the wake of the Dunkirk evacuation, Britain attempted to acquire artillery from the United States. A batch of 395 guns ordered by France but in transit at the time of the armistice was taken over by Britain in 1940. Due to the neutrality policy at the time, 500 75mm M1897 guns were sold as surplus via Bethlehem Steel. These were used to re-equip British field artillery batteries for home defence, as well as allied units including Polish and Czechoslovak units in Britain. Some guns were also provided to Canada. In British service, the gun was known as the Ordnance QF 75mm Mk 1; the improved guns with pneumatic tires were designated as Mk 1*. A special pedestal mounting for conversion to coastal defence guns was developed as the Mounting 75mm Mk 1. The 75mm guns were gradually replaced as 25-pdr guns became available, and as mentioned below, some were transferred to the Free French forces in Africa in 1942.

Finland

In 1939, Finland attempted to buy field artillery from France. Due to French shortages, very little was obtained. A total of 12 75mm M1897 guns were received in March 1940. Germany sold Finland a further 36 guns in October 1940, captured during the Norwegian campaign. These guns were used mainly by coastal defence units. Besides the field guns, Finland also obtained 12

75mm antiaircraft guns on the M1915 platform mounts. As in the case of the field guns, these were used mainly in coastal defence units. All of these guns were badly worn out and most were retired in 1942.

Due to the need for better antitank guns, in February 1943, Finland attempted to acquire the 7.5cm PaK 97/38. Germany agreed to modernize the Finnish guns into this configuration, and all 60 Finnish 75mm guns were shipped off to Germany for rebuilding. Many of the guns were too badly worn for conversion and, in the end, some 46 antitank gun conversions were returned to Finland where they were dubbed the 75 PstK 97-38. They were nicknamed *Mulatti* (*Mulatto*) and saw extensive combat use in the 1944 Continuation War against the Red Army.

A 75 PstK 97-38 in Finland, in combat near Ihantala on June 30, 1944 against the Soviet 30th Guards Tank Brigade. A Soviet T-34 tank can be seen burning on the road in the background after this gun hit its thinner rear armour. (SA-kuva/CC-BY-4.0)

France (post-1940)

Following the 1940 armistice, Vichy France was permitted to maintain an army in the North African colonies. There was a clandestine effort starting in 1941 to improve the local arsenals. The 63e Régiment d'artillerie d'Afrique in Fez created a Groupe speciale d'artillerie consisting of 75mm guns on naval pedestal mounts and mounted on the rear beds of commercial trucks. At least four of these were built. Also, at least one gun-armed train was built by French naval personnel for port defence in Morocco. Some of these guns saw combat in November 1942 during the Operation *Torch* landings by the US Army.

Gen Pierre Koenig's 1er Brigade Forces françaises libres (FFL: Free French Forces) was equipped with about 40 75mm guns from British stocks, mainly American-modified guns on the M1897A4 carriage with the Martin-Parry motorization upgrade. The brigade had an artillery regiment with four batteries of 75mm guns (six each) and an antitank company with a further six guns. In addition, French mobile columns had a number of commercial

The French Navy assembled an improvised artillery train for coastal defence near Casbah de Mehdia west of Port Lyautey in Morocco. The guns were mounted on standard pedestal mounts that were used by the French Navy for both warships and coastal defences. This train defended 'Green Beach' against the US Army's Task Force Goalpost, Western Task Force during the Operation *Torch* amphibious landings in November 1942.

One of the 75mm M1897A4 guns that took part in the defence of Bir-Hakeim in May-June 1942 with Gen Koenig´s 1er Brigade Forces françaises libres during the Gazala battles in Libya. These guns were part of a shipment from the United States to France in 1940 that was diverted first to Britain and later to Free French forces in North Africa.

trucks modified to carry the 75mm on their rear beds using a fixture developed by Capt Maurice Bayrou and Capt Yves Belan, and called Canon BB after the designers. During the fighting at Bir-Hakeim in May–June 1942, the French defenders claimed to have knocked out 52 German and Italian tanks, mainly with the 75mm guns.

The most sophisticated of the mobile 75mm guns was developed in May–August 1942 under the direction of S/Lt Adrien Conus.

Poland

The Polish Army first obtained the 75mm M1897 in 1917 when the French government agreed to raise Polish units in France under the command of Gen Jósef Haller. Haller's 'Blue Army' was transferred to Poland in 1919 and at the time had 180 75mm M1897 guns. Poland attempted to purchase a further 830 guns from France in 1919–20 due to the conflict with Soviet Russia. The precise number of guns obtained is not certain, but at the end of the war in November 1920, the Polish Army still had 783 75mm

G **AUTO-CANON CONUS, 3E ESCADRON, 1ER REGIMENT DE MARCHE DES SPAHIS MAROCAINS, TUNISIA, 1943**

The most sophisticated of the Free French mobile 75mm guns was developed in May–August 1942 under the direction of S/Lt Adrien Conus. This consisted of a 75mm gun on the rear of Canadian Ford CMP F30 trucks, using the turret races of knocked-out Italian M-13/40 tanks for traverse. These were fitted with armour plates by the Experimental Work Shop for the Middle East in Egypt. A dozen Conus guns were built and they equipped two platoons of the 1er RMSM. Starting in late February 1943, they were deployed with the Colonne volante (Free French Flying Column) in Tunisia, which served as flank security for the British 8th Army during the fighting along the Mareth line. They were involved in a violent series of duels with German tanks around Medenine on March 6, 1943, losing at least four of the *auto-canons*, but knocking out several German tanks

guns having lost many in combat. In Polish service the gun was designated as the 75mm armata polowa wz. 97. After the Russo-Polish War, Poland attempted to standardize its divisional field artillery batteries around the French 75mm gun while the cavalry batteries were equipped with Russian 75mm wz. 1902. A further 300 guns were purchased from France in 1924. Additional guns were acquired from other sources in eastern Europe, often by exchanging Russian field guns for the French guns. This included 28 guns from Latvia in 1924, 120 guns from Romania in 1926–30, and 69 guns from Yugoslavia in 1932–33. By 1939, there were 1,374 75mm wz. 97 guns in the Polish Army. In 1936, a programme began to modernize some guns with Michelin pneumatic tires for motorized traction using the C4P half-track prime mover. These were used in the two newly formed mechanized brigades. At the time of the September 1939 conflict, there were 1,230 75mm wz. 97 in Polish service. They were widely used during the fighting, and were particularly valued as antitank guns. Germany captured most of the surviving guns, but the Red Army also captured 346 guns.

Over the years, the Soviet Union captured French 75mm guns from Poland during the wars of 1920 and 1939 as well as from other sources including French units near Odessa in 1919 and Baltic armies in 1919–20. About 200 of these war-booty guns were sold to China in the 1930s. This particular example is still preserved at the Central Museum of the Russian Armed Forces in Moscow, though its precise origin is not clear. (Author)

Germany

The Wehrmacht captured about 860 75mm guns in Poland during the September 1939 campaign, of which 80 were transferred to the Romanian Army. About 2,440 75mm M1897 guns were captured in France in the

The Polish Army modernized a few dozen 75mm guns starting in 1937 for use by the artillery batteries of the new mechanized brigades. These are examples in use with the Motorized Artillery Battalion of the 10th Mechanized Brigade on exercise in 1938.

May–June 1940 campaign, plus a significant inventory of barrels and other gun parts. The French examples were designated as 7.5cm FK 231(f) for the basic M1897 and FK 232(f) for the 60 upgraded M97/33 that were found. These guns were often known generically as the 7.5cm FK 97(f). The Luftwaffe expressed interest in a portion of the guns for conversion into a cheap Flak force; this never materialized. The Kriegsmarine took over a few hundred guns for arming vessels assigned to Operation *Sealion*, the planned invasion of Britain. Aside from several hundred guns assigned to the army for *Sealion*, many of the rest were sent back to Germany for potential use as fortification guns, for training or as war reserve.

In 1941, the German Army faced a severe shortage of effective antitank guns when confronted by the Soviet T-34 and KV tanks. One method to quickly increase the inventory was to deploy the French 75mm guns since they had better performance than the 3.7cm PaK 36. The existing 75mm antitank rounds could penetrate 52mm of armour at 500m and 40mm at 1,500m. While not adequate against the frontal armour of the T-34 or KV, they could penetrate the side or rear armour at shorter ranges. Furthermore, the Red Army was still heavily reliant on light tanks such as the T-60. These made up nearly half the tank inventory in 1942 and they were very vulnerable to the 75mm gun.

The main drawback of the French 75mm gun was its archaic carriage that was designed for horse towing and that had restricted traverse. The solution was to mount it on a more modern carriage. The 5cm PaK 38 was being replaced by the 7.5cm PaK 40, and the PaK 38 carriage was

An example of a 7.5cm PaK 97/38, preserved for many years at the Ordnance Museum at Aberdeen Proving Ground, Maryland. (Author)

The 7.5cm PaK 97/38 saw extensive use in Russia, France and the Mediterranean coast. This particular example was captured by the US Army in Sicily, but it is unclear whether it was in German or Italian service at the time. The marking on the shield reads 'Hochstgeschwindigkeit 20km' (Maximum speed 20km), a reminder to the driver that the gun was not designed to conduct road travel at speeds greater than 20km/h.

selected for the conversion. To help reduce recoil, a special Solothurn pepper-pot muzzle brake was added. The resulting gun was designated as the 7.5cm PaK 97/38. An initial order for 1,000 conversions was placed in January 1942, and the first deliveries were made in May 1942. The 7.5cm PaK 97/38 was viewed as an inexpensive expedient, costing about RM 8,000, mainly for the PaK 38 carriage. This compared to RM 12,000 for the new 7.5cm PaK 40.

While normal solid steel shot was not entirely effective from such an old gun, the advent of shaped-charge warheads offered greater possibilities. The first of these 7.5cm projectiles, the Gr. 38 HL (Holladung: shaped charge) had been introduced in 1940 for the 7.5cm infantry gun and the short 7.5cm gun on the PzKpfw IV tank. These early shaped-charge warheads could only be fired from guns with a low muzzle-velocity. When fired from high-velocity guns, the shaped-charge warhead was usually crushed before the penetrating jet could properly form. The early shaped-charge warheads were not especially effective and so not manufactured in significant numbers.

Due to the Soviet tank threat, improved versions were introduced including the GR. 38 HL/A in May 1942 with a penetration of 70mm, the HL/B with a penetration of 75mm, and finally the HL/C with a penetration of 100mm. When fired from the French 75mm gun, this munition had an initial velocity of about 450m/s which was slow enough for the shaped charge to detonate properly. This dramatically improved the antitank potential of the French 75mm gun and so led to further conversion orders. In total, 2,854 were produced in 1942 and a further 858 in 1943 for a grand total of 3,712. In addition, a further 160 were ordered in 1943 on 7.5cm PaK 40 carriages. These were effective enough that 2.6 million rounds of special shaped-charge ammunition were produced for this gun in 1942–44.

Of these antitank guns, around 520 were exported to Germany's allies including Italy, Romania, Hungary, Finland and Bulgaria. A total of 1,411 of the German guns were reported lost in combat: 159 in 1942, 643 in 1943, 594 in 1944 and 15 in the first two months of 1945.

Inventory of French 75mm guns in German Army Service (FK 231(f) and PaK 97/38)										
7/42	1/43	2/44	5/44	6/44	7/44	8/44	10/44	11/44	12/44	3/45
898	1,847	1,493	672	635	623	590	348	190	145	122

Unlike the 7.5cm PaK 40, the Pak 97/38 was not widely used to arm Panzerjäger tank destroyers. Ten improvised conversions were made in field depots on war-booty Soviet T-26 light tanks for 3./Pz. Jäg. Abt.563 during 1943.

Aside from its use as an antitank gun, most of the remaining French 75mm guns were used for coastal defence as part of the Atlantikwall fortification programme. Some were used in their existing form from concrete Ringstand gun-pits. However, a portion were rebuilt on the *leichte Sockellafette* (light pedestal mount) which offered much better traverse as well as improved elevation for a secondary antiaircraft role. Some of these were deployed on smaller Kriegsmarine vessels and warships.

Italy

Due to a severe shortage of effective antitank guns, in 1942 the Italian Army acquired the German 7.5cm Pak 97/38 conversions. Nine batteries of six guns each were deployed with the Armata Italiana in Russia (ARMIR) but all were lost in the catastrophic defeats around Stalingrad in the winter of 1942–43. Italy also acquired a small number of French 75mm M1897, probably during the demilitarization of some French units in southern France and North Africa. These were used in a coastal defence role on Sicily, and may have been deployed elsewhere as well.

Italy confiscated a number of French guns in the North African colonies and used them to reinforce various Mediterranean defences including those on Sicily. This is a Canon de 75 *modèle 1897* Type Maroc, a modification of the normal gun but with special steel wheels to offer the gun crew better protection against rifle fire. It was deployed by the Italian Army at the Ponte Dirillo strongpoint near Gela on Sicily's southern coast where it was encountered by the US Army during Operation *Husky* in July 1943.

FURTHER READING

The magisterial history of French artillery development by Gen Challéat covers the initial development of the Canon de 75 up to 1910. Unfortunately, Challéat died before the third volume was completed. His task has been taken up by Gen Guy François in his publications, especially in the excellent French military history magazine *GBM* (*Histoire de Guerre, Blindès & Matériel*). The American side of the story is covered in Dickinson's semi-official histories. Post-World War I US developments are covered in numerous articles in the *Field Artillery Journal* in the 1920s and 1930s as well as archival records of the Ordnance Department in Record Group 156 at the National Archives and Records Administration (NARA II) in College Park, MD. Details of German development were found in the Heereswaffenamt records in Record Group 242 at NARA II.

Books

Christian Benoit, *Le canon de 75: Une gloire centenaire*, Établissement d'impression de l'armée de terre, Château-Chinon: 1996.

Jules Challéat, *L'artillerie de terre en France pendant un siècle: histoire technique (1816–1919). Tome 2,*
1880–1910, Charles Lavauzelle: Paris, 1935.

Frank Comparato, *Age of the Great Guns*, Stackpole, Harrisburg: 1965.

Benedict Crowell, *America's Munitions 1917–1918*, Government Printing Office, Washington DC: 1919.

W. N. Dickinson, *History of Anti-Aircraft Guns*, Government Printing Office, Washington DC: 1920.

W. N. Dickinson, *The Story of the 75 (75mm Field Gun)*, Government Printing Office, Washington DC: 1920.

Guy François, *Le canon de 75 modèle 1897*, Ysec, Louviers: 2013.

Michel Goya, *Flesh and Steel During the Great War: The Transformation of the French Army and the Invention of Modern Warfare*, Pen & Sword, Barnsley: 2018.

Pierre Hoff, *Les programmes d'armement de 1919 à 1939*, Service historique de l'armée de terre, Château de Vincennes: 1982.

Paweł Janicki, *Armata wz.1897 Kal. 75mm (Schneider)*, Edipresse, Warsaw: 2014.

Capt D'Artillerie Leroy, *Historique et organisation de l'artillerie: l'artillerie française depuis le 2 août*
1914, École militaire de l'artillerie: 1922.

William Snow, *Signposts of Experience: Memoirs of the Chief of Field Artillery 1918–1927*, CreateSpace, Middletown, DE: 2014.

Pierre Touzin, François Vauvillier, *Les canons de la victoire 1914–1918: Tome 1 L'artillerie de campagne*, Histoire & Collections, Paris: 2006.

n. a., *Instruction militaire: Croquis du canon de 75 Mle 1897*, Armée française, Paris: 1929.

n. a., *Le livre du gradé d'artillerie*, Lib. Militaire Berger-Levrault, Paris: 1929.

n. a., *Notes on the French 75mm Gun*, US Army, Washington DC: 1917.

n. a., *Technical Manual TM 9-305, 75mm Gun Materiel, M1897 and Modifications*, US Army, Washington DC: 1941.

n. a., *Technical Manual TM 9-1305, Gun and Carriage, 75mm, M1897, All Types, and Special Field Artillery Vehicles*, US Army, Washington DC: 1942.

Articles

Pierre-François Aujas, 'L'autocanon antiaérien de 75: un materiel emblématique,' *GBM*, Part 1: No 129, 2019, pp. 13–21, Part 2: No 130, 2019, pp. 11-22.

Gladeon Barnes, 'Our Superior Modernized 75s,' *Scientific American*, January 1940, pp. 16–18.

Eric Denis, 'La course au 75 nouveau: Bourges gagne par KO,' *GBM*, No 110, 2014, pp. 83–87.

Guy François, 'Améliorer le canon de 75?,' *GBM*, Part 1: No 105, 2013, pp. 39–48, Part 2: No 106, 2013, pp. 49–59.

Jean-Jacques Moulins, 'Les canons de 75 en défense des côtes,' *39–45*, No 226, September 2005, pp. 46–54.

François Vauvillier, '1916–18 des chenilles pour le 75,' *GBM*, No 89, 2009, pp. 68–79.

François Vauvillier, 'Des Chevaux-vapeur, I- Les pieces portées pour le 75,' *GBM*, No 88, 2009, pp. 30–39.

INDEX